# UNBLOCKING CRYPTO

## EVERYTHING YOU NEED TO KNOW ABOUT

## CRYPTO FROM KEY INDUSTRY LEADERS

**By:**

Lisa Nestor

David Sønstebø

Jason Rockwood

Marco Peereboom

Jacob Kowalewski

Rudy Bouwman

Steve Lee

Dan Wasyluk

Jag Sidhu

Sebastien DiMichele

Brad Hammerstron

Aaron Lasher

Jody Weeks

JASON PETERS, ADAM WEART, HAL DAVIS

ISBN: 9781792886195

THANK YOU! - From Our Daddies

Thank you for taking time to download our book on Amazon.com. With so many choices available to you, we are truly honored that you chose ours to add to your library. We have a simple request:

**Take time to leave us a review on Amazon.com.**

Your thoughts and opinions are invaluable to us and other readers interested in crypto and blockchain. Our hope is to continue to provide insight from other industry leaders representing a wide array of insight.

Thanks again,
Jason, Hal and Adam

# Dedication

This book is dedicated to our families and friends who have supported our dedication and interest in Blockchain and Crypto Technology.

# Contents

# Why we created this book

If you're like me, you've probably heard quite a bit about Bitcoin in the past. As much of a nerd as I am, I didn't look too much into it until a good friend kept telling me what was going on with his "investment". After reading the Bitcoin whitepaper and going further down the rabbit hole, I was hooked.

Back in mid 2017, there still wasn't a lot of information out there to make you comfortable on the entire situation. I even had a buddy of mine hold my hand to get me started since I was so worried that I would screw it all up and lose everything with the wrong click of the mouse.

I started to consume anything that would give me more information about what was out there. Podcasts, Books, Blogs....if I wasn't listening about it, I was reading about Crypto and Blockchain. There were 1600 coins/tokens...who can do the research to really understand them all? I realized I was in a losing battle.

During my constant questioning of anyone I knew to see if they had any insight about what was going on, I realized few people had any idea how to even get started and where to get more information. Not surprisingly, my business partners heard the most of my latest insights and started to get involved on their own.

Now I had a small group of very analytical people to talk to about this. You would think that even with engineering degrees, we'd be able to consume and understand everything that was going on. Boy were we wrong. We realized that there didn't seem to be many people out there that understood what was really happening.

Hence over a few beers we started to talk about what we would love to see. We wanted to find a resource that interviewed people at some of the top projects in the crypto/blockchain space and had them explain the world they are in and what they see the future to be like. As hard as we tried to find something like that, all we found were "crypto millionaires" giving their picks for what the best coins for the next 6 to 12 months were.

After lots of looking, we just said, fuck it, why can't we reach out to some of the top projects and see what they say. And this book was born....

# Overview of Crypto and Blockchain

Although Blockchain and Cryptocurrency have been around for a lot longer, you could argue that the introduction of Bitcoin was the first time it really generated any traction. After the white paper for Bitcoin was released in October of 2008, the first block was mined in early January of 2009.

Here is an interesting perspective of the price of Bitcoin since inception:

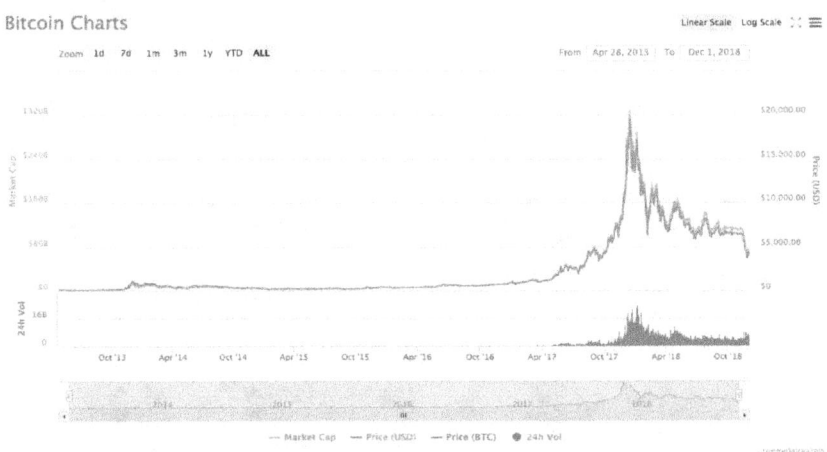

Chart Reference: www.Coinmarketcap.com

The price of Bitcoin is typically what most people talk about when they talk Cryptocurrency and while it is the largest in Market Cap and the oldest, there are still over 2000 (at the time of this writing) cryptocurriences listed on CoinMarketCap.com. And that number is still growing as there were 40 more cryptocurriencies added just last week.

In order to explain the differences between all of them, we could spend hours talking about the ways they were set up and why certain things are better than others.

## PROOF OF WORK          ## PROOF OF STAKE

The probability of mining a block is determined by how much computational work is done by the miner.

The probability of validating a new block is determined by how large of a stake a person holds (how many coins they possess).

A reward is given to the first miner to solve the cryptographic puzzle of each block.

The validators do not receive a block reward, instead they collect network fees as their reward.

Network miners compete with one another using computational power. Mining communities tend to become more centralized over time.

Proof of Stake systems can be much more cost and energy efficient than Proof of Work systems, but are less proven.

*3iQ Research Group*

Infographic Credit:

Turner Schumann
Crypto Analyst and Writer
https://www.linkedin.com/in/turner-schumann-9242b6133

The way we look at this is from a much higher level. The initial reason that cryptocurrency was formed, according to the first line of text in the Bitcoin genesis block, seems to be due to the fact that there was a loss in trust in government-backed currencies. Fast forward almost 10 years and not much has changed. Other countries are trying to get away from the US dollar and move towards gold. Trust is a common thing you will hear when you talk about Crypto. The goal of Crypto is to replace the trust needed in a 3rd party or government and utilize cryptography to secure the transaction and eliminate the need for a 3rd party altogether. If you have ever had to make a payment to someone outside your own country, you understand the pain and cost of having to deal with a trusted 3rd party.

A great article about Bitcoin came out in the New Yorker back in 2011 that provides some insight into why Bitcoin was created:

https://www.newyorker.com/magazine/2011/10/10/the-crypto-currency

Blockchain and Crypto are still in their infancy. A great look at how it compares to other financial instruments in the world is the infographic shown on the following pages:

THE MONEY PROJECT

## COMPARING THE WORLD'S
# MONEY & MARKETS

How this visualization works:  ■ ← Each square this size is worth **$100 billion**    Context on each category can be found here

---

Silver

### The World's Silver

The value of all above-ground silver stocks (est. by some at 1 billion oz) is **$17 billion** using a $17/oz spot price.

Cryptocurrency

### Cryptocurrency

The world's fastest growing asset class is cryptocurrency – but even Bitcoin looks tiny in the grand scheme of things, when compared to other global markets.

| BITCOIN $80B | THE REST $45B | ETHEREUM $37B |

Biggest Companies

BERKSHIRE HATHAWAY   MICROSOFT   ALPHABET   APPLE   FACEBOOK   AMAZON

### World's Biggest Companies

Apple is the world's largest public company by market capitalization, worth **$807 billion**.

50 Richest People

### World's Richest People

In aggregate, the world's richest people are worth a hefty **$1.9 trillion**.

| GATES $89B | BEZOS $84B | BUFFETT $81B |
| ZUCKERBERG $73B | MA $39B | MUSK $21B |

California's GDP

### State of California

America's most populous state is also an economic powerhouse with a GDP of **$2.9 trillion**. That eclipses the economies of most countries.

Fed's Balance Sheet

$3.5T Added During QE

### Federal Reserve Balance Sheet

Between 2008 and 2014, the Fed's balance sheet jumped to **$4.5 trillion** from $1 trillion due to controversial quantitative easing (QE) programs.

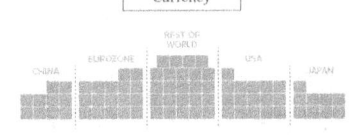

Currency

Gold

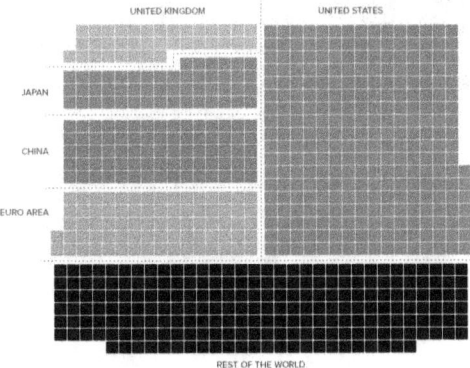

Stock Markets

### Coins & Bank Notes

The total value of all of the world's coins and banknotes is roughly **$7.6 trillion**.

### The World's Gold

The world's total above-ground gold reserves are estimated at 187,200 tonnes by the World Gold Council.

Using a $1,275/oz spot price, the world's gold is worth **$7.7 trillion**.

### Global Stock Markets

The market capitalization of all of the world's stock markets is equal to **$73 trillion**.

Global Money Supply

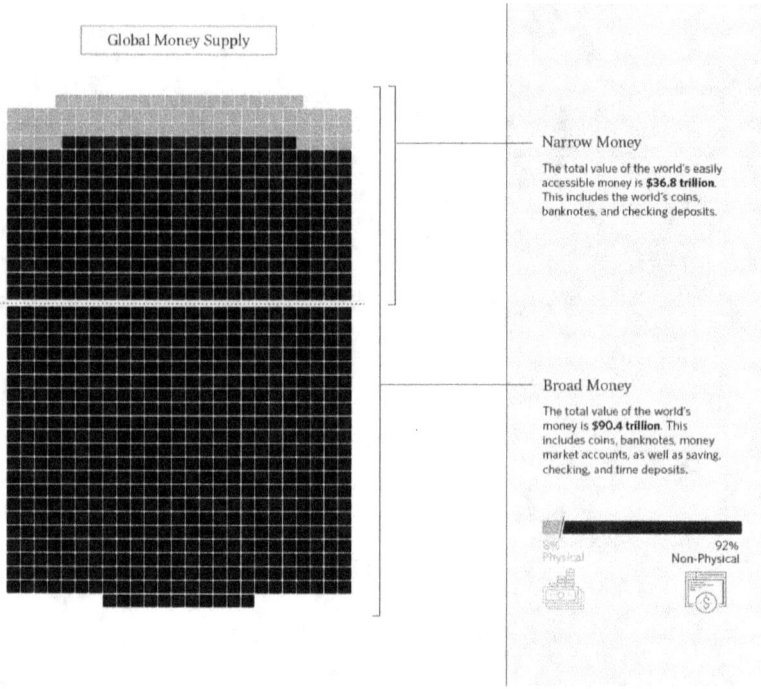

**Narrow Money**

The total value of the world's easily accessible money is **$36.8 trillion**. This includes the world's coins, banknotes, and checking deposits.

**Broad Money**

The total value of the world's money is **$90.4 trillion**. This includes coins, banknotes, money market accounts, as well as saving, checking, and time deposits.

8%
Physical

92%
Non-Physical

Global Debt

DEVELOPED MARKETS

EMERGING MARKETS

## Global Debt

This is the total amount of debt, including that accumulated by governments, corporations, and households. Together, it adds to **$215 trillion**, which is 325% of global GDP.

$70 trillion of world debt (33%) was added in the last decade globally.

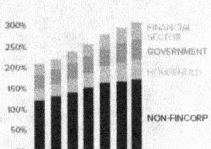

Global debt is currently at record highs, partially thanks to the sky-high expansion of credit in China.

**China: Debt as a percentage of GDP**

300%
250%  FINANCIAL SECTOR
200%  GOVERNMENT
150%  HOUSEHOLD
100%
50%  NON-FINCORP
0%  '11 '12 '13 '14 '15 '16 '17

Global Real Estate

COMMERCIAL REAL ESTATE

AGRICULTURAL REAL ESTATE

RESIDENTIAL REAL ESTATE

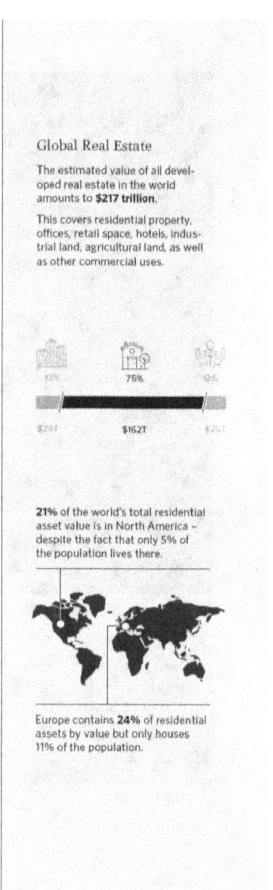

Global Real Estate

The estimated value of all developed real estate in the world amounts to **$217 trillion**.

This covers residential property, offices, retail space, hotels, industrial land, agricultural land, as well as other commercial uses.

13% — 75% — 12%

$29T — $162T — $26T

**21%** of the world's total residential asset value is in North America – despite the fact that only 5% of the population lives there.

Europe contains **24%** of residential assets by value but only houses 11% of the population.

Derivatives

LOW END ESTIMATE

## The Derivative Market

The low end estimate of the size and scope of global derivative markets is **$544 trillion** on a notional contract basis.

### What's a derivative?

A derivative is a contract between two or more parties that derives its value from the performance of an underlying asset, index, or entity.

### Examples of derivatives

- Futures contracts
- Forward contracts
- Options
- Warrants
- Swaps

Banks typically use high amounts of leverage to attain these positions. Some derivatives, such as commodity futures, are traded on regulated exchanges such as the Chicago Mercantile Exchange (CME).

However, the majority of derivatives are traded outside of exchanges between private companies, and are called "over-the-counter" trades.

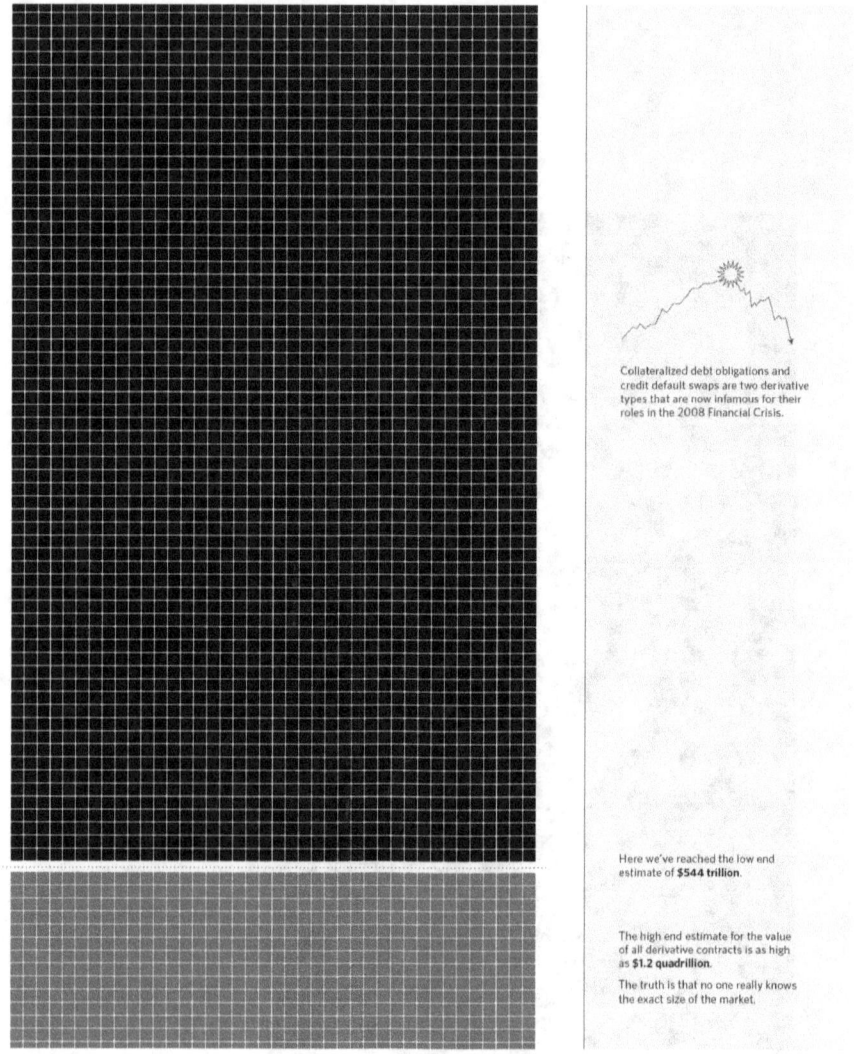

Collateralized debt obligations and
credit default swaps are two derivative
types that are now infamous for their
roles in the 2008 Financial Crisis.

Here we've reached the low end
estimate of **$544 trillion**.

The high end estimate for the value
of all derivative contracts is as high
as **$1.2 quadrillion**.

The truth is that no one really knows
the exact size of the market.

**Views on derivatives**

Many finance professionals consider derivatives to be "zero-sum" trades – in other words, there is a winner and loser on each side of the bet.

However, other experts warn that the massive size of the derivatives market could contain significant risk and consequences to global markets.

66

The positives are derivatives can be used to help allocate and take price risk out of everything from corn to cattle to stock. There are good derivatives that are self-regulating such as interest rate swaps and currency forwards. I've been working for exchanges for 41 years. I do not think regulation is incompatible with an efficient market. I think derivatives promote efficiencies.

- Dr. Richard Sandor

66

The derivatives genie is now well out of the bottle, and these instruments will almost certainly multiply in variety and number until some event makes their toxicity clear. Central banks and governments have so far found no effective way to control, or even monitor, the risks posed by these contracts. In my view, derivatives are financial weapons of mass destruction, carrying dangers that, while now latent, are potentially lethal.

- Warren Buffett

66

If there were not derivatives, there would be no bank loans at all today, because people want to get fixed-rate 30-year loans, but banks don't want to keep 30-year loans on their books.

- Jeff Greene

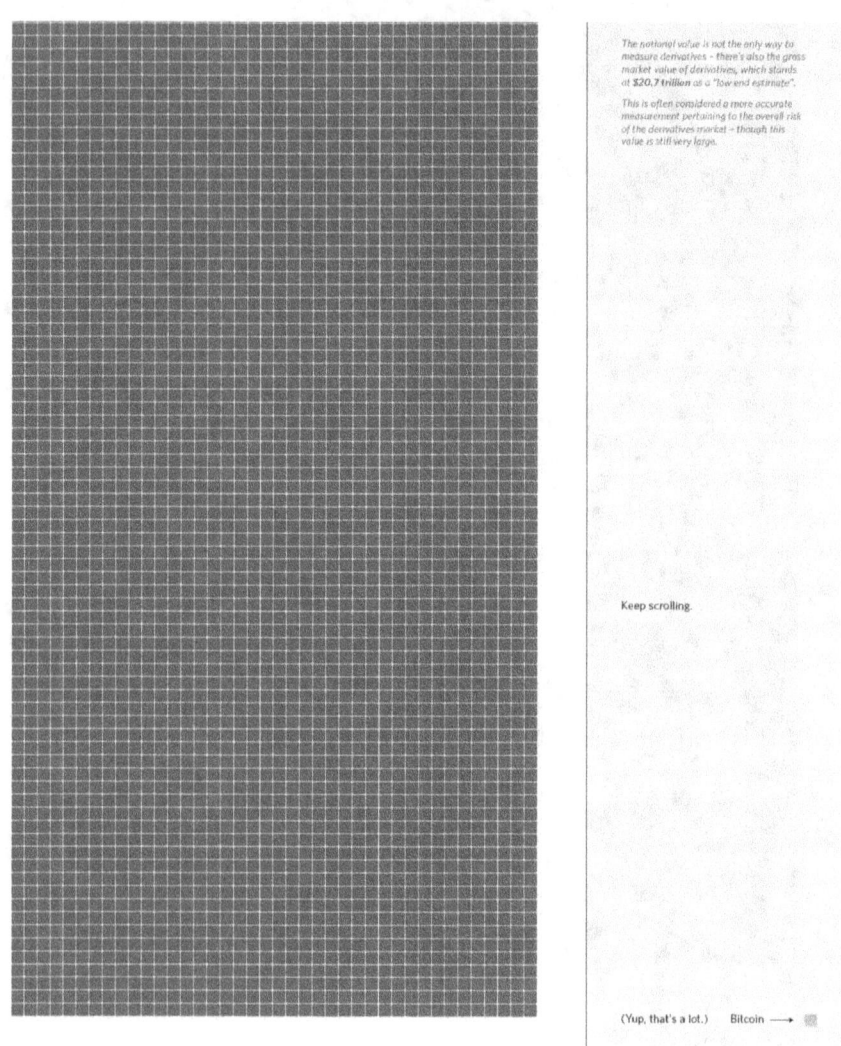

The notional value is not the only way to measure derivatives – there's also the gross market value of derivatives, which stands at $20.7 trillion as a "low end estimate".

This is often considered a more accurate measurement pertaining to the overall risk of the derivatives market – though this value is still very large.

Keep scrolling.

(Yup, that's a lot.)    Bitcoin ⟶

Infographic Credit:
**Jeff Desjardins**
*Founder & Editor-in-Chief*
Visual Capitalist
www.visualcapitalist.com

My hope is you enjoy the insights from the people that are in the trenches trying to create the future as much as I did.

# Stellar

Lisa Nestor
Director of Partnerships at Stellar.org

Lisa is the Director of Partnerships at Stellar.org, a non-profit foundation that promotes an open payments protocol to enable seamless interoperability between financial institutions, networks, and currencies. Finance is in her blood. Even before Bitcoin was around, she helped to form a micro-credit and savings institution in West Africa. Lisa is multilingual and enjoys traveling the world in her free time.

***Why is Crypto becoming more popular? What is the biggest benefit?***

Blockchain and Crypto represent new innovations that are allowing businesses, individuals, and governments to exchange value and transact with each other. This is a new type of transaction fabric available to the world and a very exciting concept. The impact it is having on development and innovation is similar to that of publicly listed securities and the growth of bonds. People are sensing that an innovation wave, wrapped around blockchain, digital assets, and cryptocurrency, will enable more access to capital and enable innovation at a global level.

It is probably safe to say that a volatile new asset like cryptocurrency with large gains and losses has created a lot of hype and excitement. Like when other major financial innovations have come to the market, you are seeing the surge due to the new asset being increasingly accessible to greater populations.

The biggest benefits are pretty simple: Faster transaction times, lower costs, and greater trust. Assuming you use an open source infrastructure, like Stellar, you are able to distribute this globally at increasingly lower costs of deployment. This will then unite different economies and markets which aren't truly connected today providing access to governments, institutions, underbanked business, and consumers.

### *What does the future of Crypto look like?*

That's a pretty big question, so I'm going to answer more in terms of what certain use cases are going to get deployed and taken forward. At a high level, it's getting past the "crypto" persona and seeing digital asset economies with a vision of centralized transaction ledgers that can be utilized for a number of different reasons (executing global payments or creating a digital realistic equity instead of having it traded).

There are a variety of application which will reach mass adoption, Stellar focuses on cross-border payments. Today if you want to provide global cross-border payment solutions for your customer, it takes a lot of work to establish the infrastructure and partnerships. There is then a high level of interaction with multiple organizations to execute within the infrastructure in order to deliver a global transaction. When we look at the companies in this space that are starting to utilize Stellar, we already see a network of financial institutions who are directly connected through our global transaction infrastructure. They issue their own digital asset to represent currency tokens that they will exchange or redeem in order to deliver a payment on behalf of an approved partner. I have seen a lot of development in and around this concept that are like stable coins, although the term of "stable coin" is still in its infancy.

The big innovation occurs in how these companies change their interactions with partners in this space. You will soon see a very interesting marketplace of payment operators who will be able to see potential partners in their space and interact with them in a much more seamless way in order to execute a transaction. This has really big implications for infrastructure overall as adoption increases and the "crypto" mindset is replaced with experience utilizing blockchain to quickly, easily, and inexpensively perform a transaction, or other use case.

I also think we're going to see a ton of innovation around other types of asset classes like securities and derivatives of securities which is exciting in terms of democratizing both investment and capital raising. I also think this will include think like community or municipal projects issuing a kind of digital claim, other bond types and assets into projects to raise funds and provide more municipal participation in these projects.

I think the future of crypto will be highly diverse with tons of applications and the blockchain is going to be the fabric that allows for that deployment, but it will really be the innovators that take that to the market.

**What is cryptocurrency's next step towards mass adoption?**

Usability is something the entire industry needs to improve on. Mass adoption is restricted until ease-of-use improves. We see Stellar as being the foundational layer of what will be a stock of application and service providers (like you would see in cloud service providers). We believe that Stellar will succeed as a protocol when we attract a diverse and rich ecosystem of application providers that build structures on top of the Stellar foundation making it easier to: deploy a Stellar node, query data, and/or perform basic infrastructure maintenance functions. Simultaneously, Steller will continue to improve as a stand up application that allows for someone to plug into the Stellar payments provider network. There needs to be layers of the stack developed around the protocols now that enable usability to a broad, but varied user base.

Standardization and clarity surrounding the different types of assets, basic regulations, and requirements about how we evaluate these different assets and asset issuers is key. Today, Stellar is a multi asset platform that has over 3,000 different assets that have been issued inside of our ledger. Asset issuers in our ecosystem consenting to a standard, say something similar to the nutrition labels on food products, for each asset will be helpful for mass adoption. We also need to make sure that the ecosystem is safe and reliable if we want to take this to the masses, which includes creating those standards and some regulatory buy-in around those standards at a global level. I think that usability and a form of standardization are two things that will take us to the adoption.

**What is the biggest surprise that will come from Cryptocurrency?**

I would say that the impacts on the global community's engagement on important policies and how individuals support and influence global policies outside of government interaction will be some of the biggest surprises to emerge. It will enable a more global society or marketplace that engages individual citizens and allows them to influence the world without geographic barriers standing in their way.

I also think the resiliency of the technology will surprise people in ways that are unexpected.

**What are you trying to achieve with your coin/token? And why are you best positioned to be the leader in this space?**

Simply stated, Stellar promotes global financial access, literacy, and inclusion by expanding access to secure, low-cost financial services. Our vision is an open, affordable, and easy to use financial system available to people of all income levels. We empower developers with useful technology to create financial products and services which fill a need in their communities.

We are a multi-asset blockchain ledger, meaning that Lumens aren't the only currency for the Stellar ledger. Although, they are the only assets in the network that do not have an issuer. This means that they are backed by the network itself. The other types of assets are used for a wide range of activities, from executing payments to issuing debt to issuing securities and bank tokens. The sky is the limit. The goal being to become the global standard that enables transactions and exchange for near free and very fast. The Lumens role is essentially to provide a small fee that's paid for transacting or submitting that kind of data into the distributed ledger. With a public ledger, you need to be somewhat thoughtful about the transactions, accounts, and trades that you are asking to report inside the ledger. The small fee helps the network be economical about those submissions and helps to protect the public network from being overly spammed.

With that being said, the real power of Lumens is that they can act as a bridge. When you have so many different types of issued assets inside the network, it's important that there is a very seamless way to be able to trade between them. An example of this would be if you had a game token and you wanted the holders of the token be able to exchange it (for fiat currency, crypto currency, or a loyalty point), it's easier to do that inside the Stellar network by maintaining liquidity between that game token and Lumens which enables a matching trade for any other asset also traded against Lumens. You can imagine if there are tens or hundreds of thousands of different types of assets inside of this ledger, making it easy to move among them is extremely valuable. This also allows Stellar to provide real time settlement between trades of different issued assets inside their network. This is extremely important when you start talking about things like payments. Stellar reduces the redundancy of capital held abroad in order to execute transactions. Today, companies have to pre-fund (keep a balance of funds in that foreign country) so that they can pay out in that currency. Stellar can reduce the float that companies hold (Example: Company A services 10 countries, so they need to maintain and manage 10 float accounts). Using Lumens provides a huge opportunity to eliminate that float by creating liquidity between Lumens and those different currency assets. This creates a more efficient way of providing liquidity in the market which enables those funds to be invested in more productive means.

**What other exciting ideas in the "crypto/blockchain" space are you paying attention to?**

I don't have a technical background, although if I asked my colleagues about this, they would say something about lightning networks or some other technical developments. On my side, I think we are pretty interested in the path forward for private ledgers that are able to deploy or transact in public ledgers. A few years ago, there seemed to be a battle between commissioned and public blockchains. It seems logical that the future ahead includes the ability for private ledgers performing private accounting (at the enterprise level or across consortiums) to do a kind of cross chain deployment or transact into public ledgers. Of course, since Stellar is a public ledger, we are keeping our eyes open to these types of developments if they make sense. There are really a lot of exciting ideas coming from this industry. Another one that comes to mind is the fundraising for municipal projects or community-based projects. Another one would be more mature trading products coming out. I think that's another really important kind of innovation down the line, especially for decentralized distributed exchanges like Stellar.

# IOTA

David Sønstebø
Co-founder and co-chair of IOTA Foundation @iotatoken

David Sonstebo is a serial entrepreneur and technology enthusiast. He was born in Norway. He is passionate about any kind of technology that can push human progress forward. David's interests are focused on Internet-of-Things (IoT), distributed ledger technologies, smart cities, digital identity, e-governance and innovative hardware design. He is the founder of IOTA, a distributed ledger technology focused on IoT, with a multi-billion dollar market cap. He was also the Founder and CEO of a stealth hardware IP start-up developing an ultra low-power processor for Internet-of-Things.

***Why is Crypto becoming more popular? What is the biggest benefit?***

Crypto's popularity is directly correlated to the digitization of our society and the emergence of data as a critical point for all transactions– consumer-facing, supply chain, healthcare, etc. Data is the new oil. The nature of Cryptocurrency's Distributed Ledger Technology (DLT) makes it the ideal way to secure and repurpose the 'new oil' and make it useful for others. In other words: it allows us to remove the data silos and create a true data lake. Crypto is the substrate that gives us untampered facts. Of course, this is a great simplification, but its basic promise (security, democratization, and removal of inefficient intermediaries) appeal to the type of society we operate in now. People want encryption, they want personalization, and they want a system that allows for collaboration without gatekeepers.

In the crypto sphere, these concepts and systems are built to be compatible and interactive, which makes it interesting to see what kind of solutions arise. One of the big benefits of IOTA's Tangle DLT is that every transaction is recorded immutably in the network. This creates a complete audit trail of what happened in the past, ensuring the future of facts. In essence, it allows you to have complete data integrity, while still remaining flexible. This opens up the development pipeline and results in the types of dynamic projects IOTA rolls out on a regular basis. Information is key in the modern economy and society as a whole. It needs to exist in the real world, not sit in a silo where a single company or entity is developing singular technology that might not be the most innovative or beneficial to all. This is what IOTA calls "permissionless innovation." Just like TCP/IP and subsequently, HTTP gave rise to permissionless innovation which resulted in the world wide web, crypto, and, more specifically IOTA, enables this Cambrian Explosion of new applications.

### What does the future of Crypto look like?

The future of Crypto will be entirely dependent on the scale of adoption and the surrounding ecosystem that drives this adoption. Most people see the intrinsic value in trustless systems. Nonetheless, until the convenience for users and developers mature, we will continue to see 'pseudo-DLTs' which are really just more of the same old shared databases with trusted gatekeepers promoting their technology as if it was a decentralized DLT. At the IOTA Foundation, we believe our Tangle DLT has the best chance to catalyze a significantly decentralized network that solves the main problems of the legacy systems, as well as early DLT technology like regular Blockchain. IOTA achieves this unique feat by enabling transactions without fees, scalability of the network and by removing the need for oligopolistic gatekeepers (i.e. miners).

Ideally, the future of crypto would see the widespread proliferation of DLT move away from first generation blockchains where you place bids to an oligopoly of validators to be able to participate in the network. This only drives the cost of network participation up. This is what the IOTA Tangle achieves by making validation of transactions an intrinsic property of utilizing the network, rather than outsourcing the validation to a third party as is the case with miners or other versions of semi-Distributed Ledgers. This is the true promise of crypto, and if we - the users - want this to become a reality, we have to accept that the first versions of blockchain were mere beta experiments.

Presuming this happens, we could see a complete overhaul of the current economic theories and business models that currently prevail in the status quo. Fee-less transactions and data transmissions that flow freely and securely without needing to trust anyone is a truly revolutionary idea. This opens up for the first time in digital payment history the ability to have a true real-time economy where you pay for the exact quantity you consume. Subscriptions and paying up front will cease, and instead, when a resource, whether it be internet, electricity, entertainment, data storage etc. is being consumed, you pay for only that and nothing more. Additionally, since transactions are only one form of data transmission, this also allows us to truly own our data and capitalize it if we volunteer to do so.

**What is cryptocurrency's next step towards mass adoption?**

At the end of 2017 and the beginning of 2018, we saw a massive exploitation of the growing hype around DLT and precisely these buzzwords: "blockchain", "decentralized", "distributed", "tokens" etc. Naturally, since most people, including company executives that are rushing to always be at the forefront to avoid obsolescence, end up in a fear of missing out state. Now that this initial bubble has finally popped, the real projects with real fundamentals underpinning them will start to emerge and prove themselves with empirical evidence, rather than hype and "castle in the sky" promises. With this comes the need for education and awareness of the technical nuances that separate real projects from hype.

Ultimately, mass adoption will only occur if we can move away from the characteristics currently limiting adoption and use– i.e. fees on transactions and the bottleneck that blockchain-based DLTs inherently have. This is absolutely paramount to having a robust, and efficient network that actually works and provides benefits over the incumbent solutions. Decentralization is not some magic formula or panacea that resolves anything on its own, in fact, it is incredibly hard to make decentralized systems user-friendly. This user-friendliness and ecosystem support is the next phase of adoption. Just like in the early days of the internet, and really any technological leap, there are early adopters which consist of genuine enthusiasts that enjoy digging deep into the nitty-gritty and getting their hands dirty. There's also the average populous who wants something that makes their life or business better in some significant capacity. It is this chasm that represents the hurdle between theory and practice.

Another element that does not get nearly enough recognition is regulation, which stems from DLT's early days where it was very driven by ideologues rather than realists. We need to be cognizant of the role that regulatory bodies can play in developing and fostering this technology. It can seem counterintuitive to put more "rules" on entities operating in a space that is trying to achieve a decentralized system, but in the end, it is the lack of accountability that leads the hype cycle of 2017 and 2018. The same was true for Internet back in the days when companies were trying to monopolize it and ISPs were fighting tooth and nails against net neutrality. This sort of regulation is conducive to growth, and it's pivotal that the DLT community embraces it rather than fight it, so that the regulators can be educated and install regulations that are informed. This is why the IOTA Foundation chose to register and set up our headquarters in Germany, which is notorious for onerous oversight. It was an arduous process, precisely because the regulations in place are not yet up to date as a consequence of simply not being informed. Done properly this will actually help to give the entire DLT space a better chance of having a favorable regulatory framework to operate within, while also filtering out bad actors that tarnish the reputation of the technology we are developing.

### What is the biggest surprise that will come from Cryptocurrency?

The biggest surprise that will come from Cryptocurrency is the different applications that we will see grow out of these systems. Right now, IOTA has projects in a myriad of verticals: mobility, manufacturing, supply chain, energy, healthcare, and the list goes on and on and grows every day. These are all areas that play a tremendous role in our everyday lives, yet most of them are still entrenched in the old legacy of having to set up complex trusted alliance structures and use outdated procedures, simply because they are 'trusted' by their overseers. By making trust implicit and inherent to these systems via DLT, efficiency will skyrocket.

Automation of these sectors is entirely dependent on this trustless nature of this technology, because at the end of the day in order for an actuator to do something autonomously, it has to act on data, and therefore it requires the ability to trust this data a priori.

For every business that has anything to do with data, which is literally every single one, IOTA is the perfect layer for data integrity and audit trails. More specifically, crypto is not just a system for exchanging goods and services, but a tool that can be used to manage autonomous vehicles, securely transfer information between manufacturing plants, provide access to data proof medical records, etc. etc. We think the general public, especially those who don't follow Crypto closely, will look back at the days of written forms of contracts, paying money to use money etc. just like we now look back on VHS and fax machines as archaic. In the end, it is just the natural progression of technology.

In terms of surprise, it will probably be in the form of realizing in retrospective reflection that we used to trust systems that weren't really trustworthy at all.

**What are you trying to achieve with your coin/token?  And why are you best positioned to be the leader in this space?**

First and foremost, unlike 99% of projects in the DLT space, the IOTA Foundation is a non-profit entity, similar to the Linux Foundation that has developed the kernel upon which most smartphones, smart TVs, routers and supercomputers, as well as a plethora of other systems, rely on today. Our mission is similar; to ensure that the best version of open source DLT becomes standardized and adopted wherever data or value transfers exist, which is virtually all of them.

Because we are an approved non-profit Foundation in a heavily regulated country we have the 'gravitas' to influence the direction that the adoption in the market takes. And, since we do not have any investors or shareholders, and the technology is entirely open source and grassroots-based, it evolves according to what is best for all, rather than compromise based on the bottom line. This allows us to be immensely flexible and operate in a way that other companies simply can't. We also have an ecosystem fund that is actively supporting projects that build open source solutions on top of IOTA. Then there is naturally the fact that the Tangle technology itself is different from regular blockchain, which resolves the pain points that have prevented real-world use cases and widespread adoption outside of speculation. Finally, as a result of the amalgam of the aforementioned benefits, we already have traction among world leading conglomerates, NGOs, governments, and start-ups, which gives the project the crucial momentum towards realizing our goal.

**What other exciting ideas in the "crypto/blockchain" space are you paying attention to?**

IOTA was born from the semiconductor and electronics realm, as we recognized how at odds old school blockchain is with hardware. So we are not paying a lot of attention to other crypto projects, besides research papers that provide valuable insight into the nitty-gritty. We are a lot more excited about the embracement of DLT from the hardware industry and companies that want to utilize the technology itself.

# VeChain

Jason Rockwood is a forward-looking digital transformation executive and former Chief Information Officer. Jason has been active in cryptocurrency and blockchain since buying Bitcoin in 2011 at $10. He was formerly Vice President of Innovation and acting CIO at the Miami HEAT and the American Airlines Arena, where he covered all aspects of enterprise IT, including application development, digital customer experience design, and IT strategy. Jason discovered VeChain in 2017, and immediately recognized its potential to transform how enterprises operate. He founded Thrudheim LLC in April 2018 as an expression of his commitment to expanding the VeChain Ecosystem and the number of companies it serves. You may follow Jason on Twitter at @jasonrockwood.

**Why is Crypto becoming more popular? What is the biggest benefit?**

At its core, blockchain is a general term for a set of technologies that distribute a data set of information across members of a community, and new data can only be added when there's a consensus across all members about the validity of new entries.

Different blockchains use different ways to achieve that consensus, hence the terms Proof of Work, Proof of Stake, Proof of Authority, etc. These protocols are different ways of "proving" that new information added to the ledger (and the entity adding it) is valid.

Because this consensus is mathematically generated, rather than consensus by human minds, the authority/validity of the information is trustworthy. A key assumption in blockchain/crypto is that math is more trustworthy than a human. Humans are error-prone and corruptible.

The world's economy runs on human trust. You trust your waiter to not spit in your food. You trust your banker to not steal your money. You trust your elected officials to not take advantage of you. And guess what?! They all do the things you trust them not to do.

Because the economy runs on human-trust, and humans can't be trusted, the economy is super inefficient. Banks charge transaction fees to cover fraud; doctors have malpractice insurance; paperwork is complicated and requires notaries, etc.

One of the most omnipresent and costly forms of trust is branding. We pay more money for branded products because manufacturers invest in brands in order for consumers to trust the products. You buy a branded item because you trust it, and you pay more for the privilege.

Blockchain is "the trust machine" because math (cryptology) is trustworthy, and humans aren't. When you take out human-based trust and put cryptographic trust in, you get data that is immutable, transparent, secure, and private. This opens up three big use cases.

The first blockchain use case is a transformation in how digital records are stored, managed, secured, and shared. Record keeping will become hyper-digitized. Anything that's stored "in a record" or "on the record" will be "trusted" via the blockchain.

Marriage licenses, death certificates, ID cards, notarized statements, legal rulings, financial statements, health records, real estate, and property/vehicle titles are just some of the records that can be secured with blockchain to reduce inefficiencies.

Take health records. Health records are so hard to manage because there's a lot of regulation that governs how that information is managed, secured, and shared in order to protect you (and your information) from being shared inappropriately by nefarious humans.

When the magical trust-machine (blockchain) is introduced to healthcare records, those records will be protected, and information sharing will be easier, cheaper, more secure. Best of all, you, the patient, will own those records--not the hospital.

The second blockchain use case is a transformation in the creation and exchange of financial assets. Bitcoin is the most obvious example. No third-party trust is required to transfer monetary value from one party to another. And the transfer is fast, secure, and transparent.

New asset classes are emerging, new ways of taking ownership and "tokenizing it" so that more people can participate in the ownership economy. This will allow for billions of people to participate in wealth-building activities that they are currently excluded from.

The third major transformation is in the use of "smart contracts". A contract is basically an agreement between two parties that govern who does what, when, under what circumstances, and at what costs. Currently, contracts are enforced via nefarious, error-prone humans.

Human-implemented contracts are terribly inefficient, costly, and prone to abuse. The average person doesn't read or understand the contracts that govern their daily activities, which leads to corporate and other abuses. See leases, website ToS, loans, lawsuits, etc.

Smart contracts essentially use cryptography to create robust "If This Then That" workflows, which make contracts automatically executable, enforceable, immutable, and secure. No more errors or abuse from untrustworthy, fallible, nefarious humans.

Smart contracts rely on "oracles", trusted data sources which provide the circumstances in which a contract gets executed. For example, a smart contract could say "If the temperature of my fish shipment drops below 20, cancel the shipment." Oracles here are IoT sensors.

A shipment of goods in a supply chain depends upon numerous ITTT contracts to ensure trust. At the national border, the customs agent says "IF fish HAS paperwork, THEN proceed AND collect customs tax." All this is currently manual, making it costly, slow, and error-prone

Blockchain replaces human fallibility with cryptological trust. By removing humans, complex supply chain contracts can be executed with far less cost, error, and abuse. Blockchain-enabled supply chain improvements mean consumers will pay less for higher-quality goods.

When you realize the degree to which blockchain will transform data sharing, financial transactions, and contract execution, you realize that blockchain is one of the greatest technological advancements in the history of human economic exchange.

### What does the future of Crypto look like?

VeChain aside, mass adoption of blockchain is inevitable. Just as TCP/IP and HTML run the internet, blockchain will run the economy, invisibly, in ways few people will understand. Nevertheless, billions will use it daily and not even know or care.

### What is the biggest surprise that will come from Cryptocurrency?

In fact, one of the most disruptive aspects of the blockchain will be in how individual users will regain their data from the large data-aggregators (Google, Facebook, Amazon, etc.) Consumers will not only own but will monetize their data back to the companies they choose.

**What are you trying to achieve with your coin/token? And why are you best positioned to be the leader in this space?**

I chose to get involved in the VeChain community (@vechainofficial) because I believe @sunshinelu24 and @NanXiaoning understand the complete transformation of the global economy that blockchain ushers in, and they are working to actualize that potential in every arena.

The VeChain team understands all transformations across data, finance, and contracts, and they are working with banks, industrial manufacturers, non-profits, logistic companies, governments, and consumer brands to make blockchain the protocol for how the world works.

Only by understanding blockchain's ability to transform data sharing, finance, and contracts can you appreciate the complexity of VeChain's vision and mission, and the passion of VeChain token holders accordingly.  It's a grandiose vision, but VeChain is making it happen.

Blockchain as a technology is transformational, but the work of transformation must be done by people on the ground. Blockchain is a tool, but I believe VeChain is most effectively wielding it, by driving adoption and making specific improvements to the Ethereum protocol.

# Decred

Marco Peereboom
New Systems Development Lead- Decred
CTO- Company Zero

Marco Peereboom is one of the founders and currently the New Systems Development Lead for Decred; a cutting-edge crypto currency that provides advancement in blockchain technology while also offering true governance. He is an avid open source developer who has been actively involved in crypto currency since 2011 working on and around several Bitcoin projects. He originated several innovations such as on-chain voting which set Decred apart from other digital currencies. He serves as the CTO of Company Zero and continues to hack on Decred's next generation digital governance tools. When not plastered in front of a screen Marco enjoys cooking, brewing, and baking.

### Why is Crypto becoming more popular? What is the biggest benefit?

There are various reasons for this and I don't think any one of them is simple.

The ideas behind crypto currencies go back decades but I do think that the financial crisis of 2008 precipitated interest beyond the cypherpunk movement. Ultimately Bitcoin made the ideas real and practical. It launched right in the middle of the crisis and the genesis block includes the following text: "The Times 03/Jan/2009 Chancellor on brink of second bailout for banks". Global markets were in free fall, people were getting laid-off left and right and friends and loved ones were losing their shirts in investment instruments. This generated interest from laypeople that previously ignored financial markets and trusted banks, governments and financial institutions to do the right thing. This combined with the fact that no one was prosecuted eroded the remaining trust in all those institutions.

Fast forward a few years where a generation of increasingly tech savvy people were being left behind and a movement was born.

At this point one cannot un-ring the cryptocurrency bell. Too many people have heard of it and are interested in becoming their own bank and taking ownership of their own financial future.

**What does the future of Crypto look like?**

I think that future of crypto is very bright but there will be a reckoning or crypto-winter first. Currently there are too many ill conceived or scam projects which is yet again eroding trust from users. We are going to have to shake out these projects before crypto can be mass adopted. I am also of the opinion that there will not be many projects that are going to survive the decade mark. Most cryptocurrencies do not have a change mechanism and process to deal with catastrophic failure/reality. Even Bitcoin is at risk here. For example, what happens if SHA256 is deprecated? This will be an existential threat to all SHA256 based currencies and they have no clear way of dealing with it. Projects like Decred do have a formal change mechanism and process to deal with hard decisions while maintaining project cohesion and preventing hard forks. Decred's governance model sets it clearly apart from all other cryptocurrencies.

**What is cryptocurrency's next step towards mass adoption?**

Crypto currencies need to be demystified. If we use an Internet analog, cryptocurrencies are at the "AOL CD" stage of user-friendliness. Usage needs to become more obvious for people and we will need some secure mobile wallets as well.

The good news is that universities around the world are taking cryptocurrencies very seriously and the next generation of developers will have heard or have even messed with crypto. The space will be unrecognizable in a few short years. These folks are going to help in boiling down crypto complexities. This is very exciting indeed.

**What is the biggest surprise that will come from Cryptocurrency?**

I think that tokenization will be a bit of a dud. Same for smart contracts. I know this an unpopular opinion, but I am not feeling it. So, the surprise will be that the hype won't translate into usable products and that traditional cryptocurrencies are going to be the ones left standing.

The other big surprise will be that people worldwide will be more economy savvy than their elders. Understanding crypto requires one to delve deeper into theory that typically would remain untouched.

Currently the gig economy businesses are for low-skill work like driving taxis, renting apartments etc. The Decred project is leading the way to extend the gig economy to high-skilled work. The best example is the Decred network itself. The project has a treasury that funds all development at this time. People that work on Decred are paid in Decred. This created its own little economy and helped distribute the coin wide. What is interesting from a macro scale is that this is all high-skilled work that is done at someone's convenience and level of availability.

**What are you trying to achieve with your coin/token? And why are you best positioned to be the leader in this space?**

Decred is engineered from the bottom-up to be long-lasting. Decred's governance sets the project apart from the rest of the space. The governance model formalizes the change process and treasury disbursement. As far as I know no one else has this value proposition and I think this is reflected by the well-known big public investors. Or as Chris Burniske & Joel Monégro from Placeholder VC said: "Decred's killer feature is good governance, and with good governance, you can have any feature you want."

**What other exciting ideas in the "crypto/blockchain" space are you paying attention to?**

There is an unending stream of things happening in the crypto sphere and is somewhat hard to keep track of it all. I typically am looking for governance related ideas that are floating around. Decred is at the bleeding edge of crypto currency development so we spend a fair amount of time designing new ideas and features.

I am really looking forward to getting the next generation of blockchain developers into the space. We could use some fresh eyes on the current problems.

# Lisk

Jacob Kowalewski @jacobkowalewski
Education Lead at Lisk @LiskHQ
Marketing Manager at Lightcurve @LightcurveHQ

Jacob has been involved with cryptocurrencies since he discovered bitcoin in 2011 while studying English Literature and Russian Language and Literature at the University of Nottingham. Since graduating Jacob has gone onto forge a stellar career in marketing pioneering tech concepts. He facilitated the acquisition of VC funding for a travel app (Tripwire), worked for one of the largest renewable energy companies in the UK (Ecovision) as well as on a philanthropic project dealing with ocean pollution and the aftermath of the refugee crisis in Lesbos, Greece (Coboat). Since acknowledging the potential of blockchain to vastly improve the impact of each of the projects he had worked on, Jacob decided to dedicate himself to the technology and its adoption full time. He joined Lisk as one of the earliest members of the marketing team and went on to create the Lisk Academy, one of the world's foremost educational platforms on blockchain technology.

### Why is crypto becoming more popular? What is the biggest benefit?

The technology behind cryptocurrencies, blockchain technology, is the answer to some of the most crucial issues that we face as a digital generation today, centering  around security, privacy and anonymity, among many others. Blockchain offers a solution to all of these problems: P2P networks, eliminating the need for central points of control; cryptography can guarantee security and immutability while returning privacy to individuals; the trustless nature of the system removes a reliance on mediating third parties. People are becoming more aware of the value of concepts like privacy, and in an unstable world, a technology that is not controlled by one entity with its own agendas truly appeals to people all over the world.

**What is crypto's next step towards mass adoption?**

The most pivotal step towards real adoption is the creation of a decisive blockchain application, or "killer dApp", that propels the technology into mainstream usage. The unique selling point of the application will be the fact that it is built on blockchain technology thereby making it distinctly better than anything else available on the market. The user experience will also need to match, or even surpass that of similar products available on the market that are not built on blockchain technology. Interoperability will also accelerate crypto's mass adoption. Currently, cryptocurrencies are generally limited to whichever network their tokens are active on: LSK to Lisk, ETH to Ethereum, ZEC to Zcash, SIA to Siacoin, etc. However, I believe that cryptocurrencies will soon become interoperable, enabling users to seamlessly utilise tokens with each. For example, paying in Bitcoin for a smart contract executed on a Lisk sidechain to anonymously send ZEC for the storage of data on the Sia platform. This step will truly facilitate the seamless everyday use of cryptocurrencies, making them a key aspect of the digital world.

**What does the future of crypto look like?**

Projects like Lisk that are currently working in the cryptocurrency space are laying the foundations for a future built upon blockchain technology. I believe that once cryptocurrencies enter mainstream use, cryptocurrency wallets will become a core component of the digital world. Not only will they be used on a daily basis for carrying out transactions but also as a means of storing value and facilitating loans, much like a bank. They could also be used as a means to store identity, auditing income and a data vault for personal information, thereby giving users full control over their personal data and privacy. Built on blockchain technology, the digital wallet will soon be the focal point of everyone's everyday life.

**What is the biggest surprise that will come from cryptocurrency?**

I think many people will be surprised by how unnoticeably blockchain will enter their realms of use. People assume that using blockchain technology is a complex process. However, the applications of the future operating on top of blockchain technology will be designed in such a way that they will look and feel like normal applications. This will allow users to easily use this powerful technology without the need for any prior knowledge of its nuances. I imagine this will come as a surprise to many users. There is also a firm belief outside of the cryptocurrency space that they are to too volatile to have an actual use. I think many people will be surprised just how quickly cryptocurrencies like Bitcoin will become one of the foremost ways of storing value in the world, much like gold today.

***What are you trying to achieve with your cryptocurrency/token? Why are you best positioned to be the leader in this space?***

Lisk is a blockchain application platform designed specifically for JavaScript developers. JavaScript is the most commonly used programming language in the world as it is one of the easiest to learn, yet extremely functional and flexible in what can be achieved with it. However, JavaScript developers find it difficult to actualise their ideas for blockchain applications as the platforms that allow the creation of such apps are generally limited to developers who use languages like Solidity, a programming language that is known to be quite rigid and difficult to learn. Essentially, they are a vastly underserved demographic. At Lisk we believe that giving these developers our SDK (Sidechain Development Kit) will open up the floodgates for this huge demographic to shape the blockchain industry and the greater world. Furthermore, the SDK allows developers to deploy their own sidechains, which are essentially entirely private and independent blockchains. This means that nothing that occurs on one sidechain will ever affect another sidechain; for example, a particularly popular blockchain application on one sidechain would never slow down the transactions on another sidechain. The entire Lisk product suite (Lisk Hub, Core, Commander and Elements) is written in JavaScript and node.js, designed specifically to be all that JavaScript developers need to bring their ideas to life. The Lisk ecosystem is built for JavaScript developers, by JavaScript developers.

**What other exciting ideas in the blockchain space are you paying attention to?**

Personally, I believe that blockchain offers a fantastic opportunity to restructure our electoral system, especially when combined with the tools that we already have for a liquid democratic system, such as our smartphones and apps, which allow users to vote on individual issues in real-time. Such systems have already been trialled, albeit without the use of blockchain technology, in countries like Argentina where El Partido de la Red, also known as the Net Party, ran for office in Buenos Aires on a promise to solely make political decisions based on the votes of citizens. Such concepts, in combination with the secure, anonymous and distributed nature of blockchain technology, have immense potential to restructure the outdated electoral systems that currently govern our lives.

# Digibyte

Rudy Bouwman is 51 years old, married and has 2 children: son 21 years old and daughter 19 years old.

Currently he is the DigiByte Chief Marketing Officer and Co-Founder of the DigiByte Awareness Team: a voluntary Community driven project to create DigiByte awareness and to encourage adoption by Marketing & PR, Outreach and Social Media. He's also a Director, and jointly shareholder, of R.L.S. International BV, a Multi-Vendor IT Service company offering full support in Europe on high-end servers & storage equipment.
People can contact him on twitter: https://twitter.com/RudyBouwman and Telegram: @RudyBouwman (https://t.me/RudyBouwman) or connect with him on LinkedIn: https://www.linkedin.com/in/rudy-bouwman-5a48065/
rudy@digibyte.io

### Why is Crypto becoming more popular? What is the biggest benefit?

I think because of some success stories from early adopters of Bitcoin, being millionaires now, people are looking for a next Bitcoin.
Especially the younger people, new in this space, are not interested in the project or the technology behind a currency, and don't do enough research.
That's a bad thing. Everyone should do proper research before investing in anything. Trading Cryptocurrencies can be very risky because
there is a lot of scam and a lot of crypto's without a working or proven project.
When you do a good research, you can find some real good working and proven projects. The benefit of the blockchain technology in general is clear:
It's secure and decentralized, no single point of failure. With dApps and Smart Contracts running on the blockchain, it will completely change the way we
process data and are making transactions today.

The benefit of the currency aspect, the Cryptocurrency, is that it can stored safely and be transfered world wide almost instantly and very cheap.

### What does the future of Crypto look like?

Today the total crypto market is about 300 billion and I think it will get to a multi-trillion market. There is a lot of institutional money on the side lines,
and once this market is finally regulated, this money will get into this market. It's just a matter of months in my opinion.
Also I think we will see a lot of scam coins and non-working projects disappearing.
So the dominance of working projects like Bitcoin, Litecoin and DigiByte will increase.

### What is cryptocurrency's next step towards mass adoption?

Regulation and easy obtaining and safe storage of Crypto's will make it easier for people to get started.
Like DigiByte having easy-to-use and very secure Android and iOs wallets in over 50+ languages to make it available to many people.
On the other hand, more and more merchants and payment processors are integrating Crypto payment solutions.
An example is UTRUST's WooCommerce Plugin that will enable 49M online stores to accept crypto payments.
So the way to mass adoption is already in process. It just takes time to get mor mature, but for sure, there is no way back.

### What is the biggest surprise that will come from Cryptocurrency?

The development of this market will continue to amaze skeptical people and many do still underestimate the consequences of implementation of Blockchain Technology in real life,
and the use of Cryptocurrency. The biggest surprise will be to see that this market will become a multi-trillion market, with Bitcoin maybe to $250.000 and DigiByte to $10 or maybe $100.
This is of course not advice to trade, but just my opinion.

**What are you trying to achieve with your coin/token? And why are you best positioned to be the leader in this space?**

When I started invested in Cryptocurrencies, I was looking for the best project in this space, and after decent research, I found DigiByte to be the best and also most undervalued Crypto. Reason of undervaluation was that DigiByte wasn't an ICO, so no company behind and therefore no money to pay for Marketing. Therefore, together with other community members we have started the DigiByte Awareness Team to power the marketing for DigiByte and create awareness and encourage adoption.

The DigiByte Foundation is an unincorporated, decentralized community dedicated to support the DigiByte global blockchain through three pillars: education, outreach, and the development of open source cybersecurity cryptographic protocol built on top of the DigiByte public blockchain.

DigiByte is being supported by a very large and decentralized community, Foundation, and Core team. We all believe in bringing open source and free to use cybersecurity solutions to the world. DigiByte blockchain is it's own public UTXO blockchain, and the first one with SegWit, MultiAlgo mining and DigiShield.

It's a 3-layer blockchain:
- Applications Layer (top layer with applications)
- Digital Asset / Public Ledger Layer (incentivizes the security of the platform)
- Core Communications Protocol / Global Network Layer (bottom that supports all infrastructure)

The DigiByte Cryptocurrency (DGB) was never an ICO (not an ERC20 token) and is being mined over time, with a max. supply of 21B in 2035.
DigiByte is the most mature blockchain: DigiByte has been operational since 2014 and is now 4.5 years old.

DigiByte is tried and tested with a provable track record. Many other blockchains have adopted DigiByte technology such as DigiShield.

It is even the Most Secure, and most decentralized blockchain: DigiByte cannot be hacked as there is no central server securing the system and instead is secured by a world-wide distributed node protocol,
so there is never a single point of failure. To hack the system, one would have to attack all 200.000 nodes at the same time; this is impossible.
This thanks to our five parallel cryptographic hashing algorithms (Proof of Work) which secure our network and make it truly un-hackable.
When comparing speed with other projects, you can see that DigiByte has the fastest blockchain: DigiByte allows for nearly instantaneous transactions (sends/receives).

15 seconds for a first confirmation. DigiByte is currently 40x faster than Bitcoin and running at 560 transactions per second (TPS) and will attain 280.000 in 2035 through stable, planned growth;
Fees are incredibly cheap with under 1/100 of a cent USD.
It is even possible to run dApps and Smart contracts on the DigiByte blockchain. On top of the DigiByte Blockchain, the Applications Layer, dApps and Smart Contracts can be built.

An example is Digi-ID, an open source free to use cryptographic identity system which could potentially eliminate usernames and passwords or even run parallel to them (www.digi-id.io).

Another example is DiguSign that allows you to securely store, notarize, validate and secure documents in the DigiByte blockchain (www.digusign.com).

**What other exciting ideas in the "crypto/blockchain" space are you paying attention to?**

We're living in exciting times, and I'm glad to be a part of this and to witness this revolution. Most exciting is to see that it will, and how it will, change the way people live today.
It's nice to see projects growing and see things really starting to happen.

I'm looking forward to the times that our own personal data will be secured by blockchain technology, and all our transactions will be secured by smart contracts running on that blockchain technology.

# Komodo

Steve Lee
Chief Marketing Officer at @KomodoPlatform

Steve Lee cut his teeth in the high-tech space working in enterprise networking and storage industries. After many years of not believing in Bitcoin, he decided to research thoroughly before drawing any conclusions. That led him down the rabbit hole and eventually into mining. Fueled by the excitement of the 2017 Bull Market, he found a way to get involved in the space by running the Marketing Department at Komodo. In his free time, you'll usually find him staying on top of the latest tech trends with Shark Tank playing in the background.

**Why is Crypto becoming more popular? What is the biggest benefit?**

Crypto is catching on for several reasons but, just as an example, you can look at where I started. A long time ago, I was a big naysayer of Bitcoin. Having really only worked in the technology sector focused on datacenter enterprise technology, I didn't really know much about the underpinnings of cryptocurrency so I dove into learning about the technical aspects of blockchain. So a little over a year ago, I decided to learn more and really dig deep. I read white papers, listened to podcasts, and watched videos, which all really made the potential of the technology clear. I started in the investment side which made we want to do a little more research and in turn got me more excited about the space and interested in trying to get involved. After understanding the technology, I determined that this had technical merit and wouldn't just be a fad, so I just had to figure out how to find an opportunity to get involved.

I think the biggest reason for the popularity is the ability to provide freedom. Things like "Banking the Unbanked," increasing transparency while also protecting privacy for individuals, and moving power away from those that have it and giving it to the people. As with most trends, the first investors were millennials and younger, tech-savvy people.

The biggest benefit is more difficult to say. A lot of people thought it was here and ready, but the reality is that every technology has an adoption curve. If you look at something like the Gartner Hype Cycle, we are in the trough. Crypto is not mainstream yet and there is still a ways to go. It won't die, but I think that only those with a strong foundation will survive. All of the opportunists will get regulated away.

**What does the future of Crypto look like?**

This is very hard to say since if you look at it from an industry perspective, so much has changed over the last several years. Back when I was investing, there were tons of ICOs and everything was mainly based on just technology. I believe that in the future, we'll see less ICOs and people will be investing less in those. Many people are looking at the security-based token offerings instead, so I expect to see more of a hybrid approach moving forward. VCs don't want to be late to the game again so they are going to be more involved earlier too.

In order to be successful, we're going to have to see more cooperation between projects. Komodo has always had a collaborative attitude, rather than a competitive one, so we're looking forward to working with other innovative projects to solve existing issues in the blockchain space.

**What is cryptocurrency's next step towards mass adoption?**

The crypto industry, in general, needs to mature before mass adoption will happen. Specifically, the issues the blockchain space needs to resolve are security, scalability, interoperability, and adaptability. 51% attacks are still occurring frequently and centralized exchanges get hacked pretty routinely. Most blockchain platforms suffer from congestion and impractically high transaction fees so it's not possible to run complex applications on the blockchain. There's still a lack of interoperability— trading from a

BTC-based altcoin to an ERC20 token requires three trades (from the altcoin to BTC, from BTC to ETH, and then from ETH to the desired ERC20 token). And there is some adaptability in blockchain but, many times, projects have recognized fatal flaws in their design and are trying to bolt on solutions to make the tech useful.

This is where Komodo stands to promote the mass adoption of blockchain. Komodo's underlying architecture has built-in security, scalability, and interop features so there's really no need to add on additional side projects to make the platform function. The whole ecosystem is protected with the power of the Bitcoin network through Komodo's delayed proof of work security mechanism. Every project receives a dedicated blockchain with independent infrastructure so the activity on one chain cannot and will not affect the performance of other blockchains in the ecosystem. Also, Komodo allows multiple blockchains to function as one while coin supply remains constant so any project can increase performance linearly whenever necessary. All the blockchains built with Komodo can verify transactions and are fungible with all the other chains in the ecosystem. Komodo's atomic swap tech creates direct peer-to-peer trading pairs between 95% of all cryptocurrencies in existence and allows traders to exchange coins without a 3rd party.

On top of all that, 2 more things that will need to happen to get mass adoption will be: People need to demand it and mainstream companies need to adopt it. Everyone understands the importance, but no one is going out and screaming about it (except for maybe IBM since most of their revenue now comes from support and services). The other big issue is that people need to start using the term blockchain instead of crypto. Blockchain is more about the technology and crypto is just a single use case.

**What is the biggest surprise that will come from Cryptocurrency?**

As regulations are established, there will be more emphasis on business maturity and the strength of technology any particular project offers. This may not be the biggest surprise but I anticipate blockchain to follow the general hype cycle that all emerging technologies go through. We're already seeing it now, and it'll start becoming clear who is driving technical innovations and the market will start consolidating even more than it already is.

Once you see that happen though, I think you'll see a huge uptick in the amount of money coming in and a big drop-off in the amount of negative coverage coming from the media. Then people will realize how legitimate blockchain tech is and there will be a large increase in investment and adoption from major companies and businesses.

**What are you trying to achieve with your coin/token? And why are you best positioned to be the leader in this space?**

Probably the biggest benefit that Komodo offers is unique multi-chain architecture. As I mentioned before, every other platform is really just a single blockchain with the ability to support smart contracts, tokens, and decentralized applications. However, all of the projects built on one of the shared-infrastructure platforms suffer from congestion, high transaction fees, and slow transaction speeds. That's why Komodo's multi-chain architecture such an enormous advantage. Every project that builds with Komodo's tech gets a dedicated blockchain, independent infrastructure, and, since Komodo supports tokenization and dAppps, the opportunity to build their own platform. Someone could build the whole of Ethereum with Komodo's tech, if they wanted. There's really no limit to what can be accomplished.

An example that most people might understand:  Imagine having a fiber internet connection coming into an apartment building, but just 1 router to handle all the traffic. This would obviously lead to very inconsistent bandwidth. Everyone would be able to get online at once but the internet would be so slow that it would be practically unusable. This is how the shared-infrastructure platforms work. Komodo's model is different because we give you your own fiber connection and your own wireless router. You don't have to share with anyone so you're free to use the internet at full speed, as much as you want. This is how Komodo's architecture is superior.

In the past, to launch your own blockchain you'd either have to fork an existing chain or build your own from scratch. Either way, it's an extremely difficult and time-consuming process. And, once you did launch your own chain, the hash rate would likely be so low that you'd be extremely vulnerable to 51% attacks and other manipulations. If you wanted to avoid the trouble of creating and securing your own chain, you could build on a shared-infrastructure platform. This would certainly make the process easy and you'd automatically receive security, but you wouldn't be able to grow or scale your project to any reasonable degree. You'd also be locked in to that platform and isolated from the blockchain industry outside of the platform you built on.

Komodo's architecture really solves all of these problems in one shot. You get your own blockchain with independent infrastructure so there is no congestion. Komodo provides all of the security, scalability, and interoperability you need to grow and be successful. Plus, there's no vendor-lock in and projects can operate with complete autonomy. The Komodo team is constantly developing new features and technologies, all of which are automatically pushed throughout the entire ecosystem.

Komodo's goal is to redefine what a platform should be and I think we're executing on this well.

**What other exciting ideas in the "crypto/blockchain" space are you paying attention to?**

Security Tokens. Komodo is in the process of creating our own. Most of the wall street guys are trying to create their own. Most of them will need to be regulated by the government. There are lots of new companies going after this space since it could replace the equity model (think stock market) which would then provide a lot of credibility.

Education. People really need to understand how to research. When projects talk about 1M transactions/sec without showing anything concrete, that's a problem. Investors need to be educated and all this pump and dump stuff needs to stop to improve confidence.

Komodo. We are always trying to push to the next big thing.

# Syscoin

Dan Wasyluk is the CEO of Blockchain Foundry and co-founder of the Syscoin project, a decentralized cryptocurrency. With over 15 years of enterprise software development experience, Dan first became involved with blockchain technology in 2013. In August 2014 he helped launch the Syscoin public blockchain. Dan holds a Bachelor of Science from the Rochester Institute of Technology.

Jag Sidhu is the CTO of Blockchain Foundy and a co-founder of the Syscoin project, a decentralized cryptocurrency, as well as its current lead developer. As an expert in blockchain technology, Jag also specializes in machine learning, artificial intelligence, client/server development and distributed systems with nearly 20 years of software development experience. Jag holds a Bachelor of Technology, Computer Science, from the British Columbia Institute of Technology.

Sebastien DiMichele is Co-Founder and Director of Public Relations at Blockchain Foundry and co-founder of the Syscoin cryptocurrency. Sebastien has 19 years of experience in the Telecommunications industry, from Service and Quality assurance to his last role as Project Manager, specializing in Service Delivery Carrier Relations. Sebastien was first involved in blockchain projects in 2013 and in August 2014, he helped launch the Syscoin public blockchain and has since been contributing efforts to the success of the project.

Brad Hammerstron is Co-Founder of the Blockchain Foundry and currently the Marketing Director for Syscoin. When he isn't helping to create a disruptive technology, you can find him playing music on his guitar or riding his motorcycle, depending on the weather in Canada.

### Why is Crypto becoming more popular? What is the biggest benefit?

DW
Distributed ledger technology is becoming more popular because it is a new and innovative field that has the potential to disrupt many

traditional industries in the same way the internet disrupted industries years ago. The biggest benefit to distributed ledger (aka: blockchain) technology is the immutable and transparent ledgering of data state and the ability to share that state amongst multi parties without 100% trust.

JS

Sovereignty of money and value transfer. Remove central actors from permissioned economy to free markets. It is a better form of money and market will always gravitate towards efficiency especially if it is a paradigm shift such as crypto.

SD

Crypto continues to gain popularity because of its volatile nature (many dream of striking it rich) and its underlying nature of being able to disrupt almost any industry. Celebrity endorsements, interest from large corporations, government initiatives have also brought many new traditional investors that had not previously dared to venture into the controversial industry. The immediate biggest benefit is to disrupt the current, however, I believe that the truly biggest benefit will be when governments use the blockchain for all their infrastructures.

BH

Political and financial corruption, control and manipulation are global issues, and cryptocurrency is a solution. Just as the Internet now provides globally accessible educational opportunities for anyone willing to learn, cryptocurrency now provides globally accessible financial opportunities for anyone willing to work. We're already seeing these opportunities having effects in many countries. People who previously have had little to no hope for a future in some third-world countries are now turning to the internet to learn a skill they can sell globally, to earn cryptocurrency that they can use to escape their current circumstances.

There are also VAST use-cases for the underlying blockchain technology. Not only can monetary value benefit from an unhackable cryptographic network, but information can as well. Nearly every industry on earth will be using cryptocurrency and some form of blockchain technology within the next 20 years.

### What does the future of Crypto look like?

DW

As blockchain technology gains adoption it will start to permeate many aspects of day to day life. You'll be able to buy your coffee using a blockchain-connected app on your phone, you'll be able to breeze through customs using a blockchain-based identity. You'll be able to validate the credentials of people you work with through the blockchain, important agreements will be ledgered and possibly even executed on the blockchain, etc. These systems will become more and more usable to the point where consumers won't realize they are interacting with a blockchain but can't imagine a world without the transparency and trust the blockchain provides.

JS

Borderless money plus global identity and application layers that are built on top benefiting from technology, saving time, money, fraud and bad actors from stealing or colluding

SD

Traditional paper currency will be seldom used and eventually replaced with cryptocurrencies. Unforgeable Blockchain-based Identities will replace traditional identification. Corporations will do most of their business on the blockchain, considerably reducing the possibility to hide fraudulent activity. Most governments will exclusively use the blockchain for their infrastructures providing provable transparency to its citizens; permits, licenses, voting, etc.

BH

20 years from now cryptocurrency will be completely mainstream as it is simply a superior form of money. Blockchain is still in its infancy but, just like any new technology such as the internet, the auto industry, electricity, television, radio etc. out of many, many startups, a few main projects will survive to rule the space.  Ethereum, Bitcoin and Hyperledger look to be taking the lead but many other projects can eke out their space.

**What is cryptocurrency's next step towards mass adoption?**

DW

There are currently several hurdles that for blockchain applications to gain mass adoption. The first and foremost is usability and security- while the technology itself is very secure its still too hard for people to interact with, and too easy to lose your money if you're not careful. Scalability and speed are some of the other major hurdles for the technology at this stage.

JS

Scalability and interoperability.

SD

Becoming seamless and easy-to-use is imperative for mass adoption. I consider crypto to still be at its infancy stage and it currently is still fairly difficult for non-technical individuals to get involved with cryptocurrencies. Syscoin's Alias system was the first step towards this ease-of-use, providing an "Alias" (similar to a username) on the blockchain, users don't need to remember a long 30+ random character address to receive funds; users only need to provide their Alias. Eventually, blockchain use will be seamless to 99% of the planet and will simply become the networks that corporations and governments use for everyday transactions.

BH

Time and education. It is unreasonable to think that any technology with such clear benefits or such massive investment can fail. Making blockchain or cryptocurrency simple to understand, and easy to use is a clearly defined goal of many projects and necessary for mass adoption.

**What is the biggest surprise that will come from Cryptocurrency?**

DW

How it starts getting used in day to day life and provides utility beyond simple value transfer.

JS

I think everything besides money that works at scale will need government top-down permissioned

SD

I believe that all cryptocurrencies combined will soon surpass one trillion dollars and will eventually surpass all combined markets that exist today.

**What are you trying to achieve with your coin/token? And why are you best positioned to be the leader in this space?**

DW

SEE JAG ANSWER

JS

Value in industry by providing sovereign money but application layers built on top with speed (zdag) and flexibility in mind (smart contracts). Smart cities become possible. We offer something no one else does with speed and flexibility.

SD

Syscoin has been at the forefront of blockchain innovation since its launch in 2014. At launch, we released the world's first decentralized marketplace, using a combination of hardened smart-contracts designed for the Syscoin platform. Our team is a partner of Microsoft and we are members of the Decentralized Identity Foundation (DIF).

In 2016, our team founded Blockchain Foundry Inc. a publicly-traded Canadian blockchain consultancy and software development corporation and we have been building solutions using the Syscoin blockchain and developed Blockmarket Desktop; an easy-to-use portal to Syscoin's decentralized marketplace. The Syscoin platform provides a unique token-creation system, offering a low-cost and scalable alternative to Ethereum's smart contract platform. One of the latest versions of Blockmarket Desktop now provides a built-in token creation system and is now the fastest, lowest-cost and easiest way to create a token on the blockchain.

BH

Syscoin has two goals:

One is to create a global marketplace based on cryptocurrency. This not only uses cryptocurrency but the underlying architecture is based on blockchain technology. This eliminates the middleman, political interference and high fees of other global marketplaces. This will offer a globally accessible fair trade platform for anyone, anywhere on Earth. Amazon/Ebay and other marketplace systems currently take up to 25% of profits directly away from the merchant and consumer and use draconian practices against merchants to steal their markets and profits. Syscoin eliminates infrastructure costs by offering a powerful global network that is freely accessible with 100% uptime. This allows anyone with anything to sell to get into cryptocurrency without the barrier of entry. And with the population of the world holding a video camera in their hand, and a clickable screen, the opportunities for buying and selling across all forms of media are astounding. Imagine watching a movie and being able to click on any product shown in the background and being able to research and buy it or being able to snap a video of your car and instantly list it for sale. Syscoin is the only blockchain project with the entire suite of contracts ready-built to handle a global marketplace, and the only one fast enough and scalable enough to handle it.

Two: Syscoin offers an entire platform for blockchain development similar to Ethereum with pre-made smart contracts that satisfy 75% of business use-cases, instant transactions scalable far above Visa speeds, trustless escrow and a platform for making custom cryptocurrencies, tokens and assets with ease. We are currently approaching many government institutions to offer blockchain based solutions for many government services to eliminate corruption, increase efficiency, speed and democratic power and opportunity back in the hands of their populations. Syscoin is also developing a next-level blockchain to cover the rest of the use-cases not currently possible with any current Blockchain platform.

**What other exciting ideas in the "crypto/blockchain" space are you paying attention to?**

DW

Work being done in the scalability and speed arena- things like casper and plasma. Alternative solutions teams are exploring to achieve scaling and speed on the blockchain. Governance models around distributed ledger technology are also very interesting. New proofs such as proof-of-storage and proof-of-replication.

JS

Zero knowledge proofs, sharding techniques, crypto economic models for flexible applications on blockchain (smart contracts/dapps)

SD

There are thousands of exciting "ideas" in the blockchain space, the use-cases for blockchain technology is constantly increasing and there is a handful of truly-innovative projects out there that are will certainly change the world. The ICO aspect of the industry, however, has attracted many projects that are simply in it for the financial aspect of the ICO; at least 90% of ICOs do not make it to market; exercising your own in-depth due diligence on any project is completely essential. What currently excites me most, however, is adoption and investments from large corporations and governments which will pave the way for mass adoption.

BH

I look at projects that see a larger picture, like Blocknet which is making a blockchain router to connect ALL the blockchains, or projects that use the element of time as a new dimension in their projects. You will see massive changes to music and entertainment in the future based on blockchain technology and time. New opportunities for artists to prove ownership, to share, to collaborate and to share without risk of theft or needing a legal team.

# BRD

Aaron Lasher is an early bitcoin investor and co-founder of the popular crypto wallet, BRD, a company on a mission to be the world's largest decentralized financial institution. BRD has customers in over 150 countries who use the app to store billions of dollars worth of digital assets. In a past life, Aaron was an offshore sailing captain, completing a circumnavigation of the globe from 2006–2008. Today, he never misses an opportunity to use nautical references when discussing bitcoin, drawing from his many encounters with dysfunctional economies in far-off countries.

*Why is Crypto becoming more popular?*

People are slowly waking up to the fact that there is a parallel financial system that serves them better than the one they use today.

*What is the biggest benefit?*

The ability to store and control your money, without borders or restrictions, is highly empowering. This means your funds will never be blocked, locked, scrutinized, or confiscated. It makes life more predictable and free.

*What does the future of Crypto look like?*

A bumpy road to a place where the largest currencies are as stable and integrated as modern fiat, without the downside of inflation.

*What is cryptocurrency's next step towards mass adoption?*

Some smaller sovereign nations will begin accumulating bitcoin as a part of their treasury fund allocation. This will kick off a period of legitimization and further demand from larger countries that follow.

**What is the biggest surprise that will come from Cryptocurrency?**

We get surprised every day. Although we have no idea what big surprises are in store, we expect them. But they wouldn't be surprises if we knew what they are in advance!

**What are you trying to achieve with your coin/token? And why are you best positioned to be the leader in this space?**

We are aiming to engineer a loyalty and rewards program that puts common programs such as air miles and hotel points to shame. We are best positioned to do this because we focus on business viability as a first priority, to support resource allocation to token utility and benefits.

**What other exciting ideas in the "crypto/blockchain" space are you paying attention to?**

Mainly focusing on taking a piece out of retail and investment banking at the moment, but many on our team are involved in a variety of side projects or consultancies in their (meager) free time.

# OTHERS IN THE CRYPTO INDUSTRY

## Miners

Jody Weeks
People can reach out to Jody via Facebook or
www.WeeksAbroad.com
They can join Bitclub at www.Bitclub.Network/Joby

### Why is Cryptocurrency becoming more popular? What is the biggest benefit?

Cryptocurrency equals financial freedom and inclusion for all. Freedom has always been popular among people all over the world. The biggest benefit is inclusion for everyone, transparency, prosperity, speed, security, privacy, a hedge against inflation, immutability, and the freedom to transact with whomever you want, anywhere in the world without having to ask a bank or government for permission.

### What does the future of Crypto look like?

Crypto will dominate as more and more people realize that they can become their own bank and have control over their own finances.

### What is cryptocurrency's next step towards mass adoption?

Education. That is where Bitclub comes into play. We have been building an army of crypto currency evangelists who are sharing this technology with their friends and loved ones who in turn do the same. 3 tell 3 who tell 3 who tell 3 and pretty soon millions of people get exposed to it! We have figured out a way to pay people to do what they are ALREADY currently doing for free. i.e. Spreading the message of Bitcoin and the blockchain!

**What is the biggest surprise that will come from Cryptocurrency?**

Dollars/Euros/Yens and Pounds finance the military industrial complex. Bitcoin does not. Governments and banks will start to lose power. They won't be able to murder as many people as they do now. This will be a great thing for humanity. The world will be surprised to see the all the abundance and prosperity that happens when humanity is living in peace and free. When all human interactions are voluntary. Where people respect the non-aggression principle. Meaning they don't use force, fraud or coercion to get their way. What a wonderful world it will be!

**What scares you the most about cryptocurrency? What excites you the most?**

What scares me most is the volatility. Smart people buy low and sell high. However, when the masses of uneducated new comers enter the space they may do stupid things, like buy high and then sell low. When that happens, people lose money... People who lose money become negative and talk poorly about it to their friends. Hackers who steal from people and exchanges also leave a bad taste in people's mouth.
Remember the story about the Goose that laid the Golden Egg? Bitcoin is the "golden egg" Many people are buying the eggs... Next week they are still buying eggs... and next month, they are still having to buy eggs... Im most excited about being able to buy the "goose that lays the golden egg" I think its way smarter to buy the goose. Wouldn't you agree? That's what you do when you join Bitclub. Mining Bitcoin is the "Goose that lays the golden eggs."

**Why is use case so important? Will the average person really use different coins based on different use cases or are certain coins only ever going to be an investment tool?**

Most coins will be SECURITIES like stocks certs are today. It will make investments more liquid and speed everything up. That's what Tzero is all about! Settling those transactions fast!
I think there will probably only be 10 crypto CURRENCY coins that are used by the masses world wide. I'd like to see the coins that get mass adoption be the Monero, Zcash, Dash and PIVX coins because of the privacy aspect of them but I also realize Governments around the world are probably going to start putting pressure on the exchanges to de-list those coins because governments believe that you are their slaves, that you are their property. They want to tax you so as to fund their Welfare/Warfare state.
If everyone used Zcash for instance and stopped paying taxes and using fiat currencies that the government of the world keep printing and printing and printing... how would those governments continue to finance their mass murder and genocide? I'm sure government would still find a way because the masses of economic and historically illiterate people falsely believe they are free... or worse, they believe that they need government to rule over them... taking care of them from cradle to grave...

**What is the most exciting project or projects that are you paying attention to?**

I set a goal to create 1000 millionaires before I die. Thus far Bitclub has over 110 members making $100,000 a month or more. That's more than $1m a year! Paid out in Bitcoin! So, we are well on our way! It's VERY exciting to give people, who are stuck living paycheck to paycheck, trying to make ends meet, a way to EARN Bitcoin by helping us crowd fund the data center. The "Bitcoin Mines" that we are building around the world.

I'm also in the middle of tokenizing water. I believe water is one of the most important resources humans need to thrive. Currently a gallon of water is selling for more than a gallon of gasoline... It shouldn't be like that... We have a plant-based water bottle that disintegrates which will help clean up our oceans. So were calling it H2 Zero! Zero plastic, Zero fluoride, Zero contaminates etc.

I'm also working on some disruptive energy technologies that turn heat into electricity. This will free humanity from the grips of the oil cartel and will help us use less electricity in our mining operations.
I'm also working on bringing Cannaceuticals to the marketplace. Things like CBD so that we can keep people healthy and off prescription drugs.

Freeing humanity from the grips of the banking cartel, the oil cartel and the pharmaceutical cartel has been my mission for the last 20 years. I would love for you to join me if you feel led! Together we can make the world a much better place for our children to inherit.
Another project that I invested in that will be huge is called www.ColdStorageCoins.com

We sell physical gold/silver/copper coins with crypto loaded to them.
It's going to be a great way to bridge the old world to the new world.

# Epilogue – What we learned

After trying to do my own research in the last year and a half, I feel like I was able to get just as much of the important data in spending less than 1 hour reading the responses in this book.

A lot of the terms in this book went quite a bit over my head, although after doing a little extra research I came to an understanding. I'm glad that there are people that not only understand them but are working to try to implement them.

While Crypto was the main focus, Crypto is just a small part of what Blockchain actually is. Crypto is the hot topic and easy to understand how to utilize it. Blockchain is going to continue to transform multiple industries in the near future though.

Crypto still has a little way to go in terms of the user interface to make things simpler. The good news is there are a lot of companies that agree and are focused on that.

It's a movement that can't be stopped at this point. Not only are the benefits more useful but due to the decentralization of a lot of these, it will be hard to ever stop completely.

The future is bright, although we are still not exactly sure how long it will take to get to stronger immersion. There are so many interesting use cases that are really creating almost a digital revolution.

This latest bear market for cryptocurrencies had put a little bit of a question mark on if things would really survive. After reading the insights from the authors, I feel much more confident that the near future will be focused around Blockchain technology and our lives will be much better because of it.

# Resources

## Exchanges
- Coinbase https://www.coinbase.com/
- Binance https://www.binance.com/en
- Bittrex https://bittrex.com/
- Poloniex https://poloniex.com/
- Kraken https://www.kraken.com/

## Other options
- Changelly https://changelly.com/
- Uphold https://uphold.com/en

## Where to go for research
- Coinmarketcap - https://coinmarketcap.com/
- Wallet Investor - https://walletinvestor.com/

## What to use for storage
- Nano S - https://www.ledger.com/
- Trezor - https://trezor.io/

## Other
- A great primer on what money actually is, Mike Maloney's Hidden Secrets of Money: https://youtu.be/DyV0OfU3-FU
- What part of the world is using Bitcoin in real time: http://www.fiatleak.com/
- If you want help calculating taxes on your Crypto: https://bitcoin.tax/
- If you want to trade using multiple exchanges in 1 location: https://www.coinigy.com/

# Acknowledgements

THANK YOU!

This book wouldn't be possible without the talented people working on the next generation of crypto and blockchain projects. In a world where everyone is overloaded with too many tasks and not enough time, these people saw the vision and shared their insights. Our thanks go out to them dealing with our calls and emails to try to get everything "perfect".

www.ingramcontent.com/pod-product-compliance
Lightning Source LLC
Chambersburg PA
CBHW071218220526
45468CB00002B/650